THE WORLD SERIES

by Shane Frederick

CAPSTONE PRESS
a capstone imprint

Capstone Captivate is published by Capstone Press,
1710 Roe Crest Drive, North Mankato, Minnesota, 56003.
www.capstonepub.com

Copyright © 2019 by Capstone Press, a Capstone imprint. All rights reserved. No part of this publication may be reproduced in whole or in part, or stored in a retrieval system, or transmitted in any form or by any means, electronic, mechanical, photocopying, recording, or otherwise, without written permission of the publisher.

Library of Congress Cataloging-in-Publication Data is available on the Library of Congress website.
ISBN: 978-1-5435-9197-2 (hardcover)
ISBN: 978-1-4966-5786-2 (paperback)
ISBN: 978-1-5435-9203-0 (eBook PDF)

Summary:
Discover the legendary players, thrilling games, and long history of the World Series.

Image Credits
Associated Press: 13, 15, 17, 21, Mark Duncan, 22, Rusty Kennedy, 29; Dreamstime: Jerry Coli, 6, 9 (top); Getty Images: New York Daily News Archive, 26, Transcendental Graphics, 7; Library of Congress: 10 (top); Newscom: AFLO Sports, 18, Everett Collection, 24, 25, Icon SMI/Sporting News Archives, 9 (bottom), MCT/Ron T. Ennis, 12, USA Today Sports/Jayne Kamin-Oncea, 10 (bottom), USA Today Sports/Richard Mackson, cover, ZUMA Press/Keith Birmingham, 5; Shutterstock: Sam Chadwick, 1

Design Elements: Shutterstock

Editorial Credits
Editor: Gena Chester; Designer: Sarah Bennett; Media Researcher: Eric Gohl; Production Specialist: Spencer Rosio

All internet sites appearing in back matter were available and accurate when this book was sent to press.

Printed and bound in the USA
PA99

Table of Contents

CHAPTER 1
We Are the Champions 4

CHAPTER 2
The Teams 8

CHAPTER 3
The Players 14

CHAPTER 4
The Moments 20

Glossary 30
Read More 31
Internet Sites 31
Index 32

Glossary terms are **bold** on first use.

CHAPTER 1

We Are the Champions

George Springer had an October for the ages in 2017. The Houston Astros' outfielder had 11 hits over seven games. It was his first World Series. Eight of his hits went for extra bases, a World Series **record**. Five of those hits were home runs. Only two other players in history had hit five homers in a World Series.

In Game 7, Springer drove in two runs and scored twice. The Astros won 5–1. They were the champions, and Springer was named the Most Valuable Player (MVP) of the World Series.

George Springer of the Houston Astros hits a two-run homer during the 2017 World Series.

The World Series is the championship of Major **League** Baseball (MLB). There are two leagues in the MLB. They are the American League and the National League. Each league has 15 teams. After the **regular season**, each league goes through its own **playoffs**.

League playoffs decide the National League and American League champs. Those two teams meet in the World Series. The first team to win four games out of seven is the World Series champion.

The first World Series was played in 1903. The American League's Boston Americans won the championship. They defeated the National League's Pittsburgh Pirates. Several years later the Americans became known as the Red Sox.

This sign, which honors Boston's 1903 World Series title, hangs at Fenway Park. The park is the home field of the Red Sox.

Fans swarm the field after Game 1 of the 1903 World Series.

Game 7

Thirty-nine World Series have come down to the final Game 7. Five of those series have gone to extra innings to decide the winner. In 2016, the Chicago Cubs faced the Cleveland Indians in an extra-inning Game 7. Cubs right fielder Ben Zobrist hit a double in the 10th inning to finally finish the game. The Cubs beat the Indians 8–7.

CHAPTER 2

The Teams

New York Yankees

The New York Yankees have won more World Series titles than all the other teams in the MLB. Star players such as Babe Ruth, Joe DiMaggio, Mickey Mantle, and Derek Jeter have helped them win 27 championships. The Yankees won their first title in 1923. They've been winning ever since.

The Yankees earned the nickname Bronx Bombers because their hitters were so good. They won five World Series titles in a row from 1949 to 1953. They won four in a row from 1936 to 1939. From 1998 to 2000, they won three straight. They won their 27th title in 2009.

Fast Fact!

The Oakland Athletics are the only team besides the Yankees to win three straight championships. They won in 1972, 1973, and 1974.

Yankees pitcher Mariano Rivera closes Game 5 of the 2000 World Series. Rivera was a relief pitcher for the Yankees for 17 seasons.

Yankees player Joe DiMaggio touches home plate in the 1950 World Series against the Philadelphia Phillies.

The Boston Red Sox (pictured) beat the New York Giants in the 1912 World Series. The series went to eight games because the two teams ended Game 2 with a tied score of 6–6.

Red Sox third baseman Eduardo Núñez (middle) celebrates winning the 2018 World Series with his teammates.

Boston Red Sox

The Boston Red Sox were the team to beat in the 2000s and 2010s. Between 2004 and 2018, they won four championships. David Ortiz was a powerful force with his bat. Dustin Pedroia's glove and pitchers such as John Lester and David Price gave the Red Sox a solid **defense**.

In total, the Red Sox have won nine World Series. But before 2004, there was a long wait between championships. Boston won in 1903, 1912, 1915, 1916, and 1918. The great Babe Ruth helped them win three of those early titles. Ruth was sent to the Yankees in 1920. After that, the Red Sox didn't win another World Series for 86 years.

Fast Fact!

While the Red Sox went a long time between championships, Chicago Cubs fans went even longer. In 2016, the Cubs won their first World Series championship since 1908. Cubs fans had waited 108 years for it.

St. Louis Cardinals

The St. Louis Cardinals have won 11 World Series. Their total is a National League record. Their total is second in baseball history behind the Yankees' 27 titles. St. Louis won its first championship in 1926.

Star player Stan Musial was one of the greatest hitters of all time. He led the Cardinals to three championships in the 1940s. Speedy base-stealer Lou Brock and hard-throwing pitcher Bob Gibson helped win two World Series in the 1960s.

Slugger Albert Pujols, star catcher Yadier Molina, and pitcher Chris Carpenter helped bring the Cardinals championship titles in 2006 and 2011.

The 2011 St. Louis Cardinals wait at home plate for teammate David Freese (23). He hit the winning home run in the 11th inning. The Cardinals went on to win Game 7 and the championship.

Cardinals player Enos Slaughter slides across home plate to score the winning run. The Cardinals beat the Boston Red Sox 4–3 to win the 1946 World Series.

Cross-Country Winners

A handful of teams have won World Series championships for different cities. The Athletics have nine championships. The first five came when they were in Philadelphia. The other four have come since the team moved to Oakland. The Giants have eight titles. They won five in New York and three more in San Francisco. The Dodgers won once in Brooklyn and have five championships since moving to Los Angeles. Finally, the Braves have won a championship for Boston, Milwaukee, and Atlanta.

CHAPTER 3

The Players

Yogi Berra

Yogi Berra was a catcher for the New York Yankees. People think he was the funniest player in baseball. He was known for silly sayings such as "It ain't over 'til it's over."

But Berra was also known as a winner. No one played in more World Series or won more championships than Berra. He played 18 seasons in the MLB. In that time, he went to 14 World Series and won 10 titles.

Berra still holds the record for all-time most hits in the World Series. Twelve of his 71 hits were home runs.

Yankees star Yogi Berra shows off his powerful swing in a 1955 game. Berra was added to the Baseball Hall of Fame in 1972.

Reggie Jackson

Reggie Jackson was so good he had a candy bar named after him. It was called the Reggie! bar. He always seemed to get better in the World Series, which is played in the fall. That earned him the nickname "Mr. October." Jackson helped his teams win five World Series. Three of the five were with the Oakland Athletics and two with the New York Yankees. He won the World Series MVP in 1973 and 1977.

Jackson hit 10 home runs in five World Series games. In 1977, he hit three home runs in a single game. This helped the Yankees win the championship over the L.A. Dodgers.

Fast Fact!

The World Series MVP was first awarded in 1955. Three players have won it twice: Reggie Jackson, Cardinals pitcher Bob Gibson, and Dodgers pitcher Sandy Koufax.

Yankees player Reggie Jackson hits the first of three home runs in Game 6 of the 1977 World Series.

Madison Bumgarner throws a pitch during Game 5 of the 2014 World Series.

Madison Bumgarner

A team needs good pitchers to get to the World Series. The best pitcher on a team is called an ace. For the San Francisco Giants in 2010, 2012, and 2014, that ace was Madison "MadBum" Bumgarner.

In 2014, MadBum pitched an impressive 21 innings against the Kansas City Royals. He threw seven innings to win Game 1. In Game 5, he threw all nine innings for a **shutout**. Then in Game 7, he came out of the **bullpen** in the fifth inning to replace another pitcher. He pitched the next five innings to save the game.

In three games, Bumgarner allowed only one run and nine hits. He had 17 strikeouts and just one walk.

Fast Fact!

Yankees closer Mariano Rivera has pitched in more World Series games than any other player. He appeared 24 times and has saved a record 11 games.

CHAPTER 4

The Moments

Walk-Off Win

In World Series history, there's only been one walk-off home run in a Game 7. It happened in 1960.

The Pirates and the Yankees were tied 3–3 in the series. In a wild final game at Pittsburgh, the score was 9–9 in the bottom of the ninth inning.

Pittsburgh second baseman Bill Mazeroski stepped up to the plate. On the second pitch, Mazeroski smashed the ball over the left-field wall. He ran the bases as his teammates came out to home plate to meet him. He touched home, and the Pirates won the championship!

Two fans rush the field to congratulate Mazeroski as he rounds third base after his game-ending home run.

A Three-Run Bomb

The only other time a World Series ended on a home run was in 1993. Joe Carter hit a three-run bomb in the bottom of the ninth inning of Game 6. The homer won the title for the Toronto Blue Jays. It was their second straight championship.

Three players have hit walk-off homers in Game 6 to force a Game 7. Carlton Fisk of the Boston Red Sox blasted one over Fenway Park's high wall in the 12th inning in 1975. Minnesota Twins player Kirby Puckett hit one into the seats in the 11th inning in 1991. And David Freese of the Cardinals hit an 11th-inning walk-off in 2011.

Carter celebrates his home run as he rounds the bases. The hit won the Blue Jays Game 6 and the 1993 World Series title.

Perfection

One of the rarest things in baseball is a perfect game. That's when a pitcher doesn't allow any batters to reach a base. There are no hits, no walks, and no errors.

In 1956, the Yankees faced the Brooklyn Dodgers in the World Series. Yankees pitcher Don Larsen struggled in Game 2, but he was perfect in Game 5. Larsen struck out seven hitters in the 2–0 victory at Yankee Stadium. It wasn't just the only perfect game in World Series history, it was also the only no-hitter. The Yankees went on to win the World Series two games later.

Larsen throws a pitch during Game 5 of the 1956 World Series.

Yankees catcher Yogi Berra and pitcher Don Larsen celebrate Larsen's perfect game during the 1956 World Series.

Fast Fact!

Cardinals pitcher Bob Gibson holds the record for most strikeouts in a single World Series game. He struck out 17 batters to win against the Detroit Tigers 4–0 in 1968.

Giants center fielder Willie Mays makes an impressive catch with his back to the plate. Mays was added to the Baseball Hall of Fame in 1979.

The Catch

Defense wins championships. That's an old saying in sports. In Game 1 of the 1954 World Series, New York Giants outfielder Willie Mays showed off his glove.

The Cleveland Indians had two runners on base. The game was tied 2–2 in the eighth inning. Vic Wertz hit a long fly ball deep to center field. Mays took off running after the ball with his back to the home plate. The ball went over Mays' shoulder and into his glove for a beautiful basket catch.

Mays spun and made a great throw to the infield. The runners weren't able to advance, and the game remained tied. The Giants finally won the game on a home run in the 10th inning. Mays's amazing catch helped the Giants win the series over Cleveland 4–0.

The Error

Defense can lose championships too. In 1986, the Red Sox were up 3–2 in the series. They were facing the New York Mets. In Game 6, the Red Sox led 5–3. They were close to winning their first championship since 1918.

The Mets tied the game in the bottom of the 10th inning. Then Mookie Wilson hit a slow, rolling ground ball toward first base. Red Sox first baseman Bill Buckner moved to play the ball and end the inning. But the ball hopped through Buckner's legs and into the outfield. The Mets scored on the error and won the game.

Two nights later, the Mets won the World Series. Boston would have to wait 18 more years to finally win another World Series.

First baseman Bill Buckner leaves the field after his game-ending error.

Glossary

bullpen (bul-PEN)—a warmup area for pitchers

defense (di-FENS)—when a team tries to stop runs from being scored

league (LEEG)—a group of sports teams that play against each other

playoff (PLAY-awf)—a series of games played after the regular season to decide a championship

record (REK-urd)—when something is done better than anyone has ever done it before

regular season (reg-yuh-LUR SEE-zuhn)—the normal set of games that teams play in a year

shutout (SHUHT-out)—when a team doesn't score

slugger (SLUG-uhr)—a batter who gets a lot of hits